D1116266

# Ripley Readers

## *Learning to read. Reading to learn!*

**LEVEL ONE** Sounding It Out  Preschool-Kindergarten
For kids who know their alphabet and are starting to sound out words.

learning sight words • beginning reading • sounding out words

**LEVEL TWO** Reading with Help  Preschool-Grade 1
For kids who know sight words and are learning to sound out new words.

expanding vocabulary • building confidence • sounding out bigger words

**LEVEL THREE** Independent Reading  Grades 1-3
For kids who are beginning to read on their own.

introducing paragraphs • challenging vocabulary • reading for comprehension

**LEVEL FOUR** Chapters  Grades 2-4
For confident readers who enjoy a mixture of images and story.

reading for learning • more complex content • feeding curiosity

***Ripley Readers***  Designed to help kids build their reading skills and confidence at any level, this program offers a variety of fun, entertaining, and unbelievable topics to interest even the most reluctant readers. With stories and information that will spark their curiosity, each book will motivate them to start and keep reading.

**PUBLISHING**

**Vice President, Licensing & Publishing** Amanda Joiner
**Editorial Manager** Carrie Bolin

**Editor** Jordie R. Orlando
**Writer** Korynn Wible-Freels
**Designer** Luis Fuentes
**Reprographics** Bob Prohaska

Published by Ripley Publishing 2020

10 9 8 7 6 5 4 3 2 1

Copyright © 2020 Ripley Publishing

ISBN: 978-1-60991-442-4

For more information regarding permission, contact:
VP Licensing & Publishing
Ripley Entertainment Inc.
7576 Kingspointe Parkway, Suite 188
Orlando, Florida 32819

Email: publishing@ripleys.com
www.ripleys.com/books
Manufactured in China in January 2020.

First Printing

Library of Congress Control Number: 2019942256

**PUBLISHER'S NOTE**
While every effort has been made to verify the accuracy of the entries in this book, the Publisher cannot be held responsible for any errors contained in the work. They would be glad to receive any information from readers.

# Ripley Readers

# Trucks!

## All true and unbelievable!

RIPLEY
PUBLISHING

a Jim Pattison Company

# Honk! Honk! There are so many kinds of trucks!

# And every truck has a job to do.

# A truck has round, black wheels.

There are lights, too!
These help the driver see.

There are buttons and levers in the truck.

A wheel lets the driver steer, and pedals make the truck stop and go.

That farmer has a blue pickup truck to help him carry his crops!

# How will we move all of the big rocks?

The yellow bulldozer can push them out of the way!

Firetrucks can stop fires.
A hose on the truck sprays water.

Thank you, firetruck!

What is that smell?
It is the garbage truck!

# It will take the trash away.

There is so much white snow!

It is good that the orange snow plow can take care of the road.

Are you hungry?

A food truck has good things to eat!

# What if your car will not go? A tow truck can help!

# That red car is going for a ride!

Look at that big semi.
It can take cargo all over!

There are more than
15 million of them in
the United States!

This dump truck has a big bucket.
It can go up and down.

# There goes the dirt!

# A tanker truck can carry fuel.

# The driver must be careful on the road!

# Wow, look at the four big wheels on that monster truck!

# Do you want to ride in one?

# Ripley Readers

All true and unbelievable!

# Ready for More?

**Ripley Readers** feature unbelievable but true facts and stories!

LEVEL ONE
Sounding it out

LEVEL TWO
Reading with help

LEVEL THREE
Independent reading

LEVEL FOUR
Chapters

Sharks!

Trucks!

Pets

Shipwrecks

Weather

Horses

Bizarre Buildings

Dinosaurs!

**For more information about
Ripley's Believe It or Not!, go to www.ripleys.com**